# The Greenwoods ADD and SUBTRACT Fractions with Like Denominators

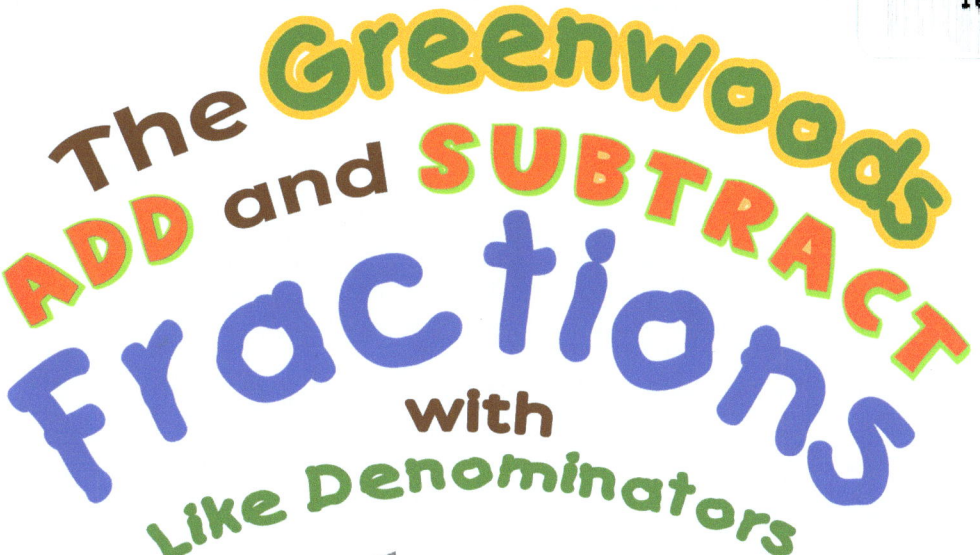

## Brandy Crump

### Illustrations by RKS Illustrations

Copyright © 2018 by Brandy Crump

All rights Reserved. This book may not be reproduced in whole or in part without the expressed written consent from the publisher, except by reviewer who may quote brief passages in a review. Nor may any part of this book be reproduced, stored in a retrieval system, or transmitted in any form or by any means, recording, photocopying, mechanical, electronic, or without the written permission of the publisher.

ISBN: 978-1-7335296-0-0

*This book is dedicated to* my baby that I miscarried in 2009. It was the pain of losing you that birthed this book series.

To my children, Myles and Bria, who inspire me to leave a legacy.

To Mr. Brown, former math teacher and coworker of 10 years, who kept asking me every single day, "Did you finish your books yet?" Well, Mr. Brown, I can finally say "YES!"

To Chris Nolen, former math teacher of 20 years and CEO of Nferno Productions, who read my manuscripts and said, "Hurry up and put those books out there!"

To the students who struggle in math and require simple explanations with examples of how it connects to their daily lives.

Today, Brea was so excited that she woke up without

an alarm; she didn't need any motivation from Mom, Dad, or her brother, Miles. In fact, she waited all summer for this day to arrive. "I am officially a fourth grader!" thought Brea. At Resilience Learning Academy, fourth graders have extra responsibilities and younger students see them as role models. "Now I'll get to be hall monitor … I'll be team leader at recess … and most importantly, I'll be going on the fourth-grade field trip," she thought as she smiled and glanced over at the clock.

Upon entering school that day, Brea's excitement turned into fear. Her forehead was sweating, hands were shaking, and her heart was beating fast. Brea finally realized that fourth grade comes with a new teacher and different classmates. "What if the new teacher is mean?

What if none of my classmates like me?" thought Brea.

All of Brea's anxiety disappeared when her fourth-grade teacher greeted her students with a warm smile and a friendly hello as she entered the classroom. Mrs. Peterson began the day with several activities that allowed her students to learn each other's names, special talents, hobbies, and sports. By the end of the last activity, Brea found a new friend named Karla, who also enjoyed swimming, gymnastics, and drawing.

After lunchtime, Mrs. Peterson taught a grammar lesson, reviewed some vocabulary

words from the third grade, and then gave a spelling quiz. Brea was ecstatic when Mrs. Peterson announced that she earned the highest score on the spelling quiz. Everything was going great until Mrs. Peterson began teaching fractions.

"Students, when adding and subtracting fractions with the same denominators, you must leave the denominators (bottom numbers) alone and add or subtract the numerators (top numbers) only," said Mrs. Peterson.

"For our first example, we will add

$$\frac{3}{5} + \frac{1}{5}.$$

Since the denominators (bottom numbers) are the same, we simply add the numerators (top numbers). So, the sum of

$$\frac{3}{5} + \frac{1}{5} \text{ is } \frac{4}{5},"$$

said Mrs. Peterson.

"Next, we will subtract

$$\frac{5}{7} - \frac{1}{7}.$$

Here again, since the denominators (bottom numbers) are the same, you only subtract the numerators (top numbers) to get 4 and leave the denominator as the same. Thus, the difference of

$$\frac{5}{7} - \frac{1}{7} \text{ is } \frac{4}{7},\text{"}$$

said Mrs. Peterson.

After demonstrating two examples, Mrs. Peterson told the class to try the next problem by themselves. The problem was

$$\frac{5}{9} - \frac{1}{9} = ?$$

After giving the class time to work on the problem, Mrs. Peterson asked Karla, Brea's new friend, to write the answer on the board. Karla went to the board and wrote 4/9—the correct answer. Mrs. Peterson thanked Karla for working at the board and asked the class if they had any questions. Brea did not understand why

$$\frac{3}{5} + \frac{1}{5} \text{ was not } \frac{4}{10}.$$

Also, she was confused about why

$$\frac{5}{7} - \frac{1}{7} \text{ was not } \frac{4}{0}.$$

However, she did not ask any questions because she was afraid that her new teacher and classmates would think she was not smart. Since none of the students asked for help, Mrs. Peterson distributed the homework, told the students to clean up around their desks, and dismissed class when the bell rang.

When Brea arrived home from school, she sat down to complete her homework. She finished her reading assignment with ease. However, she needed her big brother's help with the math.

"Miles, will you help me with my fractions worksheet?" asked Brea. "Sure, but first let me fix something to eat. You know I can't think on an empty stomach," replied Miles.

Miles set the oven to 375 degrees, took a frozen pizza from the freezer, and then cooked it for 25 minutes. Once the pizza was done, Miles called Brea over to assist with slicing it.

Miles said, "Brea, we need 3 slices for dad, 2 for mom, 2 for me, and ..." "I need only 1 slice," added Brea. "So we need a total of 8 slices," said Miles. "Guess what, Brea, we are doing fractions." Dad gets 3 out of 8 slices or $\frac{3}{8}$, mom gets 2 out of 8 slices or $\frac{2}{8}$,

I get 2 out of 8 slices or $\frac{2}{8}$,

and you get 1 out of 8 slices or $\frac{1}{8}$.

Now let's do this problem on paper.

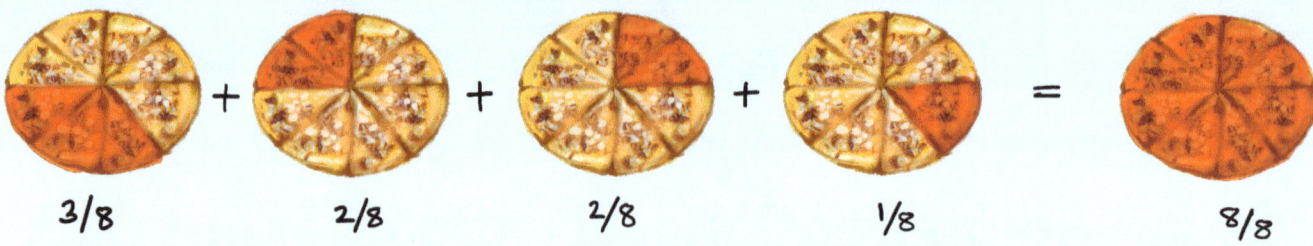

3/8 + 2/8 + 2/8 + 1/8 = 8/8

"Brother, after slicing the pizza, I understand that each slice is a part of the whole pizza and that each person gets a portion of those 8 slices. It does not make sense to add the denominators because doing so would result in us having more than 8 slices and that is impossible!" Brea exclaimed.

After finishing the pizza, Brea and Miles completed their homework and then went outside to play volleyball with their friends. During a time-out, Miles seized the opportunity to teach Brea another lesson on fractions. He called Brea and said, "There are 2 boys and 4 girls on our team. Therefore, 2 out of 6 people are boys and 4 out of 6 are girls. This can be represented with the following."

$$\frac{(2 \text{ boys})}{(6 \text{ people})} + \frac{(4 \text{ girls})}{(6 \text{ people})} = \frac{(6 \text{ people})}{(6 \text{ people})} = 1 \text{ whole team.}$$

"Once again, the denominator of 6 volleyball players remains the same because the total number of people on our team will remain the same."

During the walk back home, Brea and Miles stopped at Harvey World Mart, the local grocery store, to purchase a bag of potato chips. "Brea, we are going to buy a bag of chips for 75 cents. In my pocket, I have 4 quarters, which is 1 dollar. This situation can be represented with the following."

1 dollar  -  75 cents  =  25 cents

$$\frac{4}{4} - \frac{3}{4} = \frac{1}{4}$$

1 dollar  -  75 cents  = 25 cents

$$\frac{4}{4} - \frac{3}{4} = \frac{1}{4}$$

"Now that we have talked about 25 cents being equal to 1/4 and 75 cents being equal to 3/4, tell me what 50 cents is equal to, Brea?" asked Miles. "Oh, that's easy," replied Brea. "The 4 represents the whole dollar, so 50 cents equals 2 out of 4 quarters or the fraction 2/4." "Excellent explanation, sis! Now can you summarize the concept of adding and subtracting fractions with like denominators?" asked Miles. "Sure, brother. Basically, the denominator (bottom number) represents the whole so it stays the same. However, the numerators (top numbers) change since you either add or subtract them."

[ ] + − × ÷ = ? ( )

**Brandy Crump is the author** of a math book series which includes the following titles: (1) The Greenwoods Add and Subtract Fractions with Like Denominators, (2) The Greenwoods Add and Subtract Fractions with Unlike Denominators, (3) The Greenwoods Multiply and Divide Fractions, (4) The Greenwoods Simplify Percents, (5) The Greenwoods Add and Subtract Integers, (6) The Greenwoods Solve One-Step Equations, and (7) The Greenwoods Solve Proportions. Brandy holds a bachelor's degree in Secondary Math Education and a master's degree in Educational Administration. She has 18 years of experience in teaching mathematics to at-risk students who suffer from adverse childhood experiences (ACES). She grew up in Harvey, Illinois, and graduated from Thornton Township High School where she taught for 14 years. As the product of an underserved, poverty-stricken, and high-crime community, she experienced ACES that prepared her to better understand and connect with her delinquent and at-risk students. She has provided workshops on effective classroom management through mutually respectful relationships and increasing student engagement through cooperative groups and authentic learning activities. Brandy is a lifelong learner and continues to research best practices for reaching out to struggling students. She is a member of Delta Sigma Theta Sorority Incorporated. She enjoys working with the youth in her community, writing books, creating math games, and conducting motivational speaking engagements.

[ ] + − × ÷ = ? ( )

www.ingramcontent.com/pod-product-compliance
Lightning Source LLC
LaVergne TN
LVHW072101070426
835508LV00002B/221